Debugging & problem solving

Author: Borth, Teddy.
Reading Level: 2.4 LG
Point Value: 0.5
ACCELERATED READER QUIZ 512477

D1716929

DEBUGGING & PROBLEM SOLVING

by Teddy Borth

Cody Koala

An Imprint of Pop!
popbooksonline.com

abdobooks.com
Published by Pop!, a division of ABDO, PO Box 398166, Minneapolis, Minnesota 55439. Copyright © 2022 by Abdo Consulting Group, Inc. International copyrights reserved in all countries. No part of this book may be reproduced in any form without written permission from the publisher. Cody Koala™ is a trademark and logo of Pop!.

Printed in the United States of America, North Mankato, Minnesota

052021
092021

THIS BOOK CONTAINS RECYCLED MATERIALS

Cover Photo: Shutterstock Images
Interior Photos: iStockphoto, 5, 9 (top), 20; Shutterstock Images, 6, 9 (bottom left), 9 (bottom center), 10, 13 (top), 13 (bottom left, center, and right), 15, 16, 19

Editor: Elizabeth Andrews
Series Designer: Laura Graphenteen

Library of Congress Control Number: 2020948285
Publisher's Cataloging-in-Publication Data
Names: Borth, Teddy, author.
Title: Debugging & problem solving / by Teddy Borth
Description: Minneapolis, Minnesota : Pop!, 2022 | Series: Coding basics | Includes online resources and index.
Identifiers: ISBN 9781532169625 (lib. bdg.) | ISBN 9781098240554 (ebook)
Subjects: LCSH: Debugging in computer science--Juvenile literature. | Troubleshooting in computer science--Juvenile literature. | Problem solving--Juvenile literature. | Computer programming--Juvenile literature.
Classification: DDC 005.1--dc23

Hello! My name is

Cody Koala

Pop open this book and you'll find QR codes like this one, loaded with information, so you can learn even more!

Scan this code* and others like it while you read, or visit the website below to make this book pop.

popbooksonline.com/debug

*Scanning QR codes requires a web-enabled smart device with a QR code reader app and a camera.

Table of Contents

Chapter 1

Infestation!

Sometimes programs don't run correctly. They might **crash** or give an unexpected result. A problem in the **code** is called a bug. Changing the code to get rid of bugs is debugging.

program crash

Operation Error

Application failed. Data may be damaged.

OK

Watch a video here!

Ethan got the wrong answer on his homework. He wonders what went wrong. He goes through the question again to find the problem. He tries again to see if he gets the right answer.

Chapter 2

Try and Try Again

Josh can't remember which key opens the front door. He will try each key until the door opens. This is called "trial and error." He will keep failing until he finds the right key.

Complete an activity here!

Ella bakes cookies. Her last **batch** was too salty! This time she will try using less salt to see if that fixes the problem.

> Cookies date back almost 1,400 years. That is a lot of time to try new recipes.

Louis tries to work through a maze. If he runs into a dead end, he will try another path. He does this until he solves the maze. This is like debugging!

The largest hedge maze is in China and has nearly 5.9 miles (9.45 km) of pathways!

00011100100010011100100100110010100

dead end

Chapter 3

Finding the Problem

James is in the park. He sees there is garbage everywhere! He wants to solve the problem. James and his sister pick up the **litter**. The park will look nice!

Learn more here!

Megan's headphones aren't working. There are many things she checks to solve the problem. She tries the volume, but it doesn't help. She finds the problem. Her headphones aren't **connected**.

Chapter 4

Learning from Past Problems

Luke helps in the garden. The carrots are really big this year! He thinks about what he did different from last year. He wants to remember to do it again next season.

Learn more here!

How do you solve problems? Is there anything around you that needs debugging?

Making Connections

Text-to-Self

Have you ever had a toy that wasn't working? What did you do to fix it?

Text-to-Text

Have you read other books about debugging or problem solving? What did you learn?

Text-to-World

Can you think of a problem in your city or the world? What can your community do to solve it? What can you do?

Glossary

batch – a group of something made at one time.

code – a list of instructions that tells a computer what to do.

connect – to link two things together with a cable or wirelessly.

crash – to fail or stop running.

litter – garbage out in an open or public place.

Index

Online Resources

popbooksonline.com

Thanks for reading this Cody Koala book!

Scan this code* and others like it in this book, or visit the website below to make this book pop!

popbooksonline.com/debug

*Scanning QR codes requires a web-enabled smart device with a QR code reader app and a camera.